D1681521

AcT III
DESSERTS

The Final Curtain

Produced By

BACKERS VOLUNTEER BOARD OF THE REPERTORY THEATRE OF ST. LOUIS

ACT THREE

Proceeds from *Opening Night Entertaining* will be used to support the cultural and educational activities of The Repertory Theatre of St. Louis.

THE REPERTORY THEATRE OF ST. LOUIS
130 EDGAR ROAD
P.O. BOX 191730
ST. LOUIS, MO 63119

ALL RIGHTS RESERVED
COPYRIGHT PENDING 1993

To order copies of *Opening Night Entertaining*, send a check for $16.95 plus $1.75 for postage and handling to:

Opening Night Entertaining
P.O. Box 8014
St. Louis, MO 63156-8014

(314) 361-4419

DESIGN AND PRODUCTION
Gretchen Floresca
Crative and Design Director
Werremeyer Creative
St. Louis, Mo.

PRINTING
Fleming Printing Company
St. Louis, Mo.

PRINTED ON RECYCLED PAPER

DEDICATION

A truism of the theatre – not less true for being one – is that the stage is a cooperative art form. Unlike a chef in the kitchen who works culinary magic alone, a theatrical production is the work of many – from the stagehands to the actors, who take the bows, to the director, who captains the entire effort.

Yet a theatrical production also needs a theatre. That means the stage is really a communal effort, drawing, as do the volumes you now hold, upon the skills and work of many others besides all the theatrical professionals.

And so this dedication: for the few who take the applause; for the many who give it and their time and money; for the volunteers, the members of the Backers Volunteer Board, and everyone in between who has worked for our beloved Rep.

This book's for you . . .
and for the theatre you make possible.

> *"It was just there was some talk of dessert and I'm afraid I lost my nerve."*
>
> Woman in Mind
> ALAN AYCKBOURN

BACKERS VOLUNTEER BOARD

Ann Augustin	*Dee Laime*	*Trudie Roth*
Sue Barley	*Jean Lange*	*Sue Shapleigh*
Tina Burke	*Patti Lewis*	*Barbara Size*
Carol Chapman	*Jack Lippard*	*Betsy Smith*
Phyllis DeYong	*Barbara Mennell*	*Clare Smith*
Vi Farmer	*Marilyn Monson*	*Gwen Springett*
Mary Franckle	*Harriet Morrison*	*Marion Strachan*
Carol Gast	*Jill Norton*	*Dee Thompson*
Gloria Goetsch	*JoAnne Parrish*	*Linda Vandivort*
Louise Griesbach	*Joyce Patterson*	*William Wiese*
Vivian Kirk	*Brenda Richey*	*Janice Wohlwend*
Judy Kuhlman	*Pat Richter*	*Carolyn Woodruff*

A SOLILOQUY

No theatrical event is complete without the curtain call. It is the moment at which the audience acknowledges the work of the company and also when the actors thank the audience for participating with them in the making of a play. The call is integral to a production. How a meal finishes is also part of the whole event. From appetizer to main course to dessert—like a play—with beginnings, middles and endings—a full story is to be told. What follows are suggestions that will ensure nothing short of wild applause and shouts of "encore!" when your dinner has rung down the curtain for the moment.

Or in the words of Michael Frayn, in his fabulous play NOISES OFF, "Getting on—getting off. Getting the sardines on—getting the sardines off. That's farce. That's the theatre. That's life."

Food and theatre and life seem inextricably intertwined in the best sense.

Steven Woolf
ARTISTIC DIRECTOR
THE REPERTORY THEATRE OF ST. LOUIS

"When love and skill work together, expect a masterpiece."

JOHN RUSKIN

DESSERTS

Contents

CHAMPAGNE AND MANGO ICE WITH MINT *11*

LEMON ICE WITH CHOCOLATE-DIPPED COOKIES *12*

LOW-FAT CHOCOLATE ICE CREAM *14*
FROZEN AMARETTO SOUFFLÉ *15*

"AFTER THE THEATRE" CARAMEL CREAM AND CHOCOLATE
    SPONGE CAKE *16*

COCONUT FLAN *18*
CARAMEL FLAN *19*

CRÈME BRÛLÉE *21*

ESPRESSO CUSTARD CUPS *22*
ICED CAPPUCCINO MOUSSE *23*

MOCHA FUDGE CAKE *24*

CHOCOLATE MOUSSE *27*

CHOCOLATE PÂTE WITH PRALINE CREAM ANGLAISE *28*

CHOCOLATE TRUFFLE CAKE *30*
CHOCOLATE TRUFFLES *31*

ACT THREE

Contents

MINI-TRUFFLE CAKE WITH CHOCOLATE GANACHE
    AND FRESH RASPBERRIES *32*

WARM CHOCOLATE AND CHESTNUT TORTE *34*
WHITE CHOCOLATE CHEESECAKE *35*

DOUBLE CHOCOLATE TERRINE *36*
CHOCOLATE BREAD PUDDING *37*

FRESH FRUIT COBBLER WITH VANILLA BEAN SAUCE *38*

TROPICAL FRUIT SHORTCAKE *40*
MELTED BRIE WITH WINTER FRUITS *41*

TOASTED POUND CAKE WITH FRESH BERRIES TOSSED IN RUM SYRUP *42*
WALNUT PEAR MOUSSE WITH RASPBERRIES *43*

RASPBERRIES GRAND MARNIER *44*
RASPBERRY FLAN *45*

RASPBERRY BROWNIES *46*

CRANBERRY FOOL WITH DRUNKEN ORANGES *48*

DESSERTS

Contents

STRAWBERRIES CHAMPAGNE SABAYON *50*
STRAWBERRIES ITALIAN-STYLE WITH GRAND MARNIER CUSTARD *51*

STRAWBERRIES WITH CHOCOLATE DIPPING SAUCE *52*
STRAWBERRY ROMANOFF *53*

STRAWBERRY MARGARITA PIE WITH RASPBERRY SAUCE *55*

ROXANE'S BATTLE CAKE WITH CHOCOLATE SOUR CREAM FROSTING *56*

POPCAKE WITH PRESERVES *58*
TULIP COOKIES *59*

PLUM TART *60*

BUTTERSCOTCH BROWNIES *62*
GINGER BROWNIES *63*

CHOCOLATE PECAN SQUARES *65*

COFFEES *66*

WINES *68*

ACKNOWLEDGMENTS *69*

WINES RECOMMENDED BY:

The Cheese Place

The Wine Cellar

West End Wines

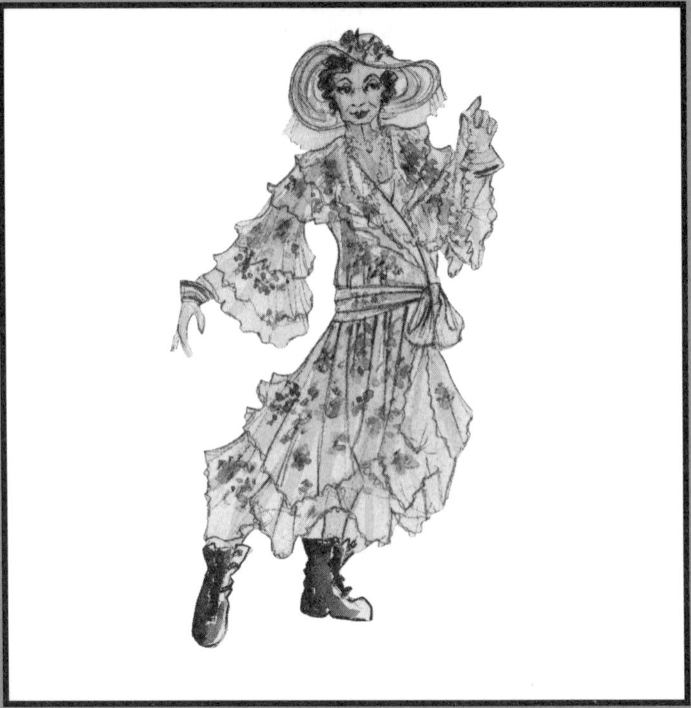

DESSERTS

Champagne and Mango Ice with Mint

SERVES 8 TO 10

3 MANGOES, PITTED AND PEELED
4 CUPS CHAMPAGNE
SUGAR, TO TASTE
1/2 CUP MINT, CHOPPED
WATER, AS NEEDED

Put mangoes and champagne in a blender. Puree until well combined. Add sugar and stir to combine. Taste and decide if you need more sugar. You want to taste the natural mango flavor. The sugar serves only to enhance. Add mint and water to thin mixture if necessary. When mixture is proper taste and texture, pour into a shallow dish and freeze. When frozen, stir well or reblend. Freeze again. The ice is ready to serve. Serve with a splash of champagne and mint garnish.

Ices are a light addition to any meal. You can get creative. The method is the same, just vary the ingredients. These are pleasing summertime flavors.

Suggested wine: Riesling

Chris Desens
The Country Club
at The Legends

Hay Fever
DOROTHY L. MARSHALL
COSTUME DESIGNER

ACT THREE

Lemon Ice with Chocolate-Dipped Cookies

SERVES 6

2 CUPS FRESH LEMON JUICE
1 CUP SUGAR
1 CUP WATER

Chocolate:
1 CUP SEMISWEET CHIPS
1/2 CUP 40 PERCENT CREAM
   WHIPPING CREAM

Combine lemon juice, sugar, and water, and chill in freezer at least 24 hours before serving.

Chocolate: In a double boiler, melt the chocolate and cream together. Stir until smooth.

Zoë Robinson, Owner
Café Zoë

DESSERTS

Cookies:

1 1/4 POUNDS UNSALTED BUTTER, SOFTENED (5 STICKS)

1/2 POUND POWDERED SUGAR

3 EGG WHITES

6 CUPS ALL-PURPOSE FLOUR

Cookies: Cream butter and sugar in a bowl. Add the egg whites and flour. Place the dough in a pastry bag and pipe the cookies onto a sheet lined with paper. Bake at 350 degrees for 15 minutes or until light brown. Sprinkle with powdered sugar and drizzle with the chocolate from a squeeze bottle.

A Day In Hollywood
A Night In The Ukraine
DOROTHY L. MARSHALL
COSTUME DESIGNER

ACT THREE

Low-Fat Chocolate Ice Cream

SERVES 8

- 1 QUART WATER
- 1 1/3 CUPS SUGAR OR SWEETENER
- 3 GELATIN ENVELOPES
- 3 TABLESPOONS UNSWEETENED COCOA
- 1/4 POUND CHOCOLATE
- 4 TABLESPOONS NONDAIRY CREAMER
- 3 EGG WHITES
- 1/2 QUART SKIM MILK
- 1 CUP YOGURT
- RASPBERRIES (OPTIONAL)

Boil water with half of the sugar. Add gelatin and bring to a boil again. Add cocoa, chocolate, creamer; stir and cool. Cook rest of sugar to soft ball (add 3 tablespoons water if necessary). In a separate bowl, beat egg whites until firm; add cooked sugar and beat at medium speed until cool. Add to chocolate mixture with skim milk and yogurt. Mix well and freeze. Serve in a glass with raspberries on top.

This is low-calorie chocolate ice cream, 34 calories per 2-ounce serving.

Suggested wine: dry sparkling wine, a Brut or Champagne

Jean Pierre Auge, Chef
Mark Twain Bancshares, Inc.

DESSERTS

Frozen Amaretto Soufflé

SERVES 12

1 TABLESPOON GELATIN
2 OUNCES AMARETTO
6 EGG YOLKS
3 OUNCES SUGAR
1 TEASPOON VANILLA
PINCH OF SALT
3 EGG WHITES
1 3/4 CUPS HEAVY CREAM
6 OUNCES AMARETTO

Bloom gelatin (until absorbed) with 2 ounces Amaretto. In a mixing bowl, add yolks, sugar, vanilla, and salt. Mix on high speed until a ribbon is formed. Transfer to mixing bowl. Heat gelatin mixture and fold into yolk base. Whip egg whites until stiff and fold into the base. Whip heavy cream on high speed. As it begins to thicken, add 6 ounces Amaretto. Remove from mixer when soft peaks can be made. Fold into the base. Transfer to a springform pan and freeze overnight. To serve, remove from freezer about 1 hour before serving and place in refrigerator. Remove from refrigerator about 5 minutes before serving.

Suggested wine: Sauternes

David Timmey
Balaban's

ACT THREE

"After The Theatre" Caramel Cream and Chocolate Sponge Cake

SERVES 12 TO 16

Chocolate Genoise:

4 OUNCES MELTED BUTTER
6 EGGS, LARGE
2/3 CUP SUGAR
1/3 CUP SUGAR
1/2 CUP CAKE FLOUR
1/2 CUP DROSTE'S DUTCH PROCESS COCOA

Caramel Cream:

2 CUPS SUGAR
1/2 CUP WATER
4 CUPS 40 PERCENT HEAVY WHIPPING CREAM

*Tim Brennan, Chef
Cravings Gourmet
Desserts, Ltd.*

Pre-heat oven to 350 degrees. Prepare 4 9-inch cake pans by spraying them evenly with Baker's Joy. Melt butter. Set aside. Warm eggs and 2/3 cup sugar in double boiler over low to medium heat for 2 to 4 minutes (do not let water touch the bottom of your bowl). Watch closely; stir regularly so as not to cook eggs! Egg-sugar mixture is ready when warm to the wrist. Mix with upright mixer for 7 minutes at medium speed (#6 setting on Kitchenaid mixer). Gradually add remaining 1/3 cup sugar while mixing. Batter should triple in volume and turn from dark yellow to pale yellow and be very frothy and thicker than when you first began mixing. Mix on high speed for 2 more minutes. Sift together the flour and cocoa until evenly blended, probably 3 times. Fold

DESSERTS

flour into the thickened egg-sugar mixture. Gently fold in the melted butter so that it's evenly incorporated without deflating the light, airy texture. (Speed and lightness of hand are essential here for a light cake). Divide among 4 9-inch cake pans (approximately 5 to 6 ounces in each). Smooth tops. Bake for 20 minutes or until springy and immediately invert on cooling rack. Stir sugar and water in 2- to 3-quart heavy saucepan over medium-low heat until sugar dissolves. (Lightweight and Silverstone will not work. A heavy saucepan is crucial for this recipe). Increase heat to high and boil without stirring until this syrup turns a deep amber color. Occasionally swirl the pan and wipe down sides with a pastry brush dipped in about 10 to 12 minutes and watch closely for last 2 to 3 minutes so as not to burn. Pour in 2 cups of cream and reduce heat to medium. It will bubble violently. Do not burn yourself on the steam it emits. Stir until smooth, then add remaining 2 cups of cream and cook 4 minutes. Remove from heat and chill overnight.

Assembly: Arrange first cake layer on serving platter. Beat caramel cream in mixer until stiff peaks form. Do not overbeat. It should look like whipped cream. Spread 1 cup of caramel cream on first layer. Smooth. Continue with the second layer of cake and the second cup of caramel cream until both are used. Chill at least 2 hours.

> *Serve after the theatre with espresso and garnish with fresh strawberries.*

ACT THREE
Coconut Flan

2 CUPS MILK
3 EGGS PLUS ONE EGG YOLK
1/3 CUP SUGAR
1/2 CUP CRÈME OF COCONUT

Thierry Meignein, Pastry Chef
The Ritz-Carlton, St. Louis

Bring milk to a boil in a saucepan and remove from heat. Mix eggs, sugar, and crème of coconut in a bowl. Add milk gradually and stir. Pour mixture into greased custard cups and place in a pan of hot water. Bake at 325 degrees for 30 to 40 minutes or until custard sets. Let custard cool and serve.

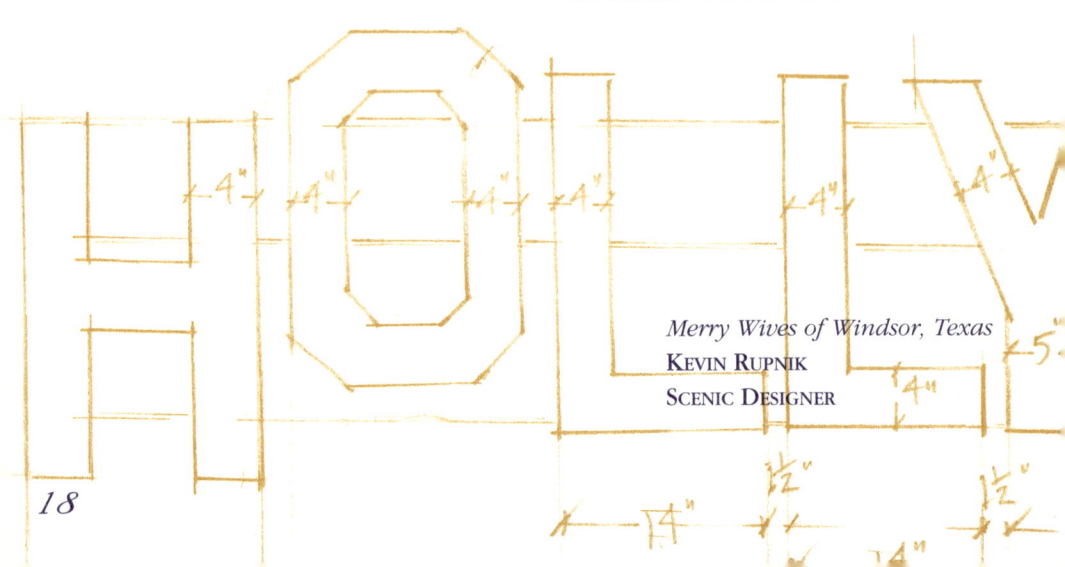

Merry Wives of Windsor, Texas
KEVIN RUPNIK
SCENIC DESIGNER

DESSERTS

Caramel Flan

1 1/2 cups sugar
Water (to cover sugar)
4 eggs
1 14-ounce can
    Eagle condensed milk
1 3/4 cups water
1/2 teaspoon vanilla
1/8 teaspoon salt
Mint for garnish
Orange segment for garnish

Sherrill Gonterman
La Chef Catering

Preheat oven to 350 degrees. Cover sugar, just barely with water. Cook in skillet over medium heat until melted and caramel-colored. DO NOT STIR! Pour into 4-ounce soufflé cups or 9-inch round cake pan. Coat bottom. Mix eggs. Add condensed milk, water, vanilla, and salt. Pour into caramelized dish. Set in larger pan. Fill pan with 1 inch hot water (water bath). Bake 40 to 45 minutes or until knife comes out clean. Chill. Turn out of pan by running knife around edge. Serve. Garnish with mint and orange segment.

Suggested wine:
a late-harvest Riesling

> "After a good dinner, one can forgive anybody, even one's relations."
>
> *A Woman of No Importance*
> Oscar Wilde

DESSERTS

Crème Brûlée

SERVES 8

2 CUPS HEAVY CREAM
1 INCH PIECE OF VANILLA BEAN

4 EGG YOLKS
3 TABLESPOONS SUGAR
4 TEASPOONS BROWN SUGAR
PINCH OF SALT

In a heavy sauce or soup pot, scald the cream and vanilla bean. Cover and let steep for 10 minutes. Remove the vanilla bean and scrape interior into cream. Set aside.

Whip egg yolks until thick and pale colored. Blend in sugar and salt. Temper hot cream into the egg yolks and sugar. Place mix in bowl over double boiler and cook until it coats the back of a spoon. Strain the mix and pour into 4-ounce custard cups. Bake in a water bath at 300 degrees for 40 minutes. Let cool several hours or overnight in refrigerator. Before serving, place 1/2 teaspoon of brown sugar on top. Spread thin layer over the surface and caramelize under the broiler.

Matthew Flatley
Dining In

ACT THREE

Espresso Custard Cups

SERVES 4

8 EGG YOLKS
1/2 CUP SUGAR
1 TABLESPOON VANILLA
1 CUP MILK
1 CUP ESPRESSO
3/4 CUP HEAVY CREAM
SAMBUCA WHIPPED CREAM

Mix yolks, sugar, and vanilla. Beat untill frothy. Scald milk and espresso. Add to eggs. Stir in cream. Bake in 10-ounce custard cups in a water bath for 30 minutes at 350 degrees. Cool and chill. May top with sambuca whipped cream.

Mike Wilson, Chef
Big Sky Cafe

Pygmalion
JOEL FONTAINE
SCENIC DESIGNER

DESSERTS

Iced Cappuccino Mousse

SERVES 8

1 CUP ESPRESSO
5 TEASPOONS GELATIN
1 CUP MILK
2/3 CUP SUGAR
2 EGGS, SEPARATED
1 TABLESPOON CORNSTARCH
1 TEASPOON VANILLA
1/4 CUP FRANGELICO LIQUEUR
1 CUP WHIPPING CREAM
WHIPPED CREAM
CHOCOLATE SHAVINGS

Chris Desens
The Country Club
at The Legends

Prepare espresso. Sprinkle gelatin on espresso to dissolve. Heat milk. In a separate bowl pour the sugar, egg yolks, and cornstarch. Whisk thoroughly, adding espresso a little at a time to produce a creamy texture. Pour this into a double boiler on medium heat. When mixture begins to thicken, add vanilla and Frangelico and allow to cool. Whisk the egg whites into soft peaks. Whip the cream and fold gently into the mixture before it sets; then fold in the egg whites. Pour into an appropriate serving dish (I use coffee cups), and freeze for at least 8 hours or until frozen. Serve with whipped cream and chocolate shavings (optional).

Suggested wine:
full-bodied red Port
or late harvest Zinfandel

ACT THREE

Mocha Fudge Cake

> "WOULD YE BOTH EAT YOUR CAKE AND HAVE YOUR CAKE?"
>
> GEORGE HERBERT

8 ounces semisweet chocolate
1 cup sugar
1 cup sweet butter
1/2 cup espresso or strong coffee
4 eggs
1/4 cup melted jelly or preserves (currant/orange marmalade)
1 cup whipping cream
1/4 cup powdered sugar
1/4 teaspoon vanilla
Fresh or candied flowers

Linda Pilcher, Chef
Something Elegant Catering

DESSERTS

Line bottom of 8 x 2 inch round cake pan or springform pan with parchment paper. Combine chocolate, sugar, butter, and coffee in pan and place over low heat, stirring until chocolate and butter are melted. Beat eggs in mixing bowl and slowly beat in slightly cooled chocolate mixture. Pour into prepared pan, filling about 3/4 full. Bake in preheated 350-degree oven for about 30 minutes, until cake cracks around sides. (Cake will be soft in the center.) Cool completely. Cover with foil and refrigerate overnight or up to one week. Loosen edge of cake with knife and invert onto plate. Trim if necessary. Spread preserves or jelly (melted) over top of cake (optional). Return to refrigerator for about 15 minutes to set. Whip cream until thick, folding in sugar and vanilla. Frost top and sides of cake with whipped cream by piping it through a pastry bag fitted with a star tip. Decorate with fresh or candied flowers, if desired.

To bake cake in 9-inch springform, prepare 1 1/2 times the recipe and proceed as above, increasing baking time as necessary.

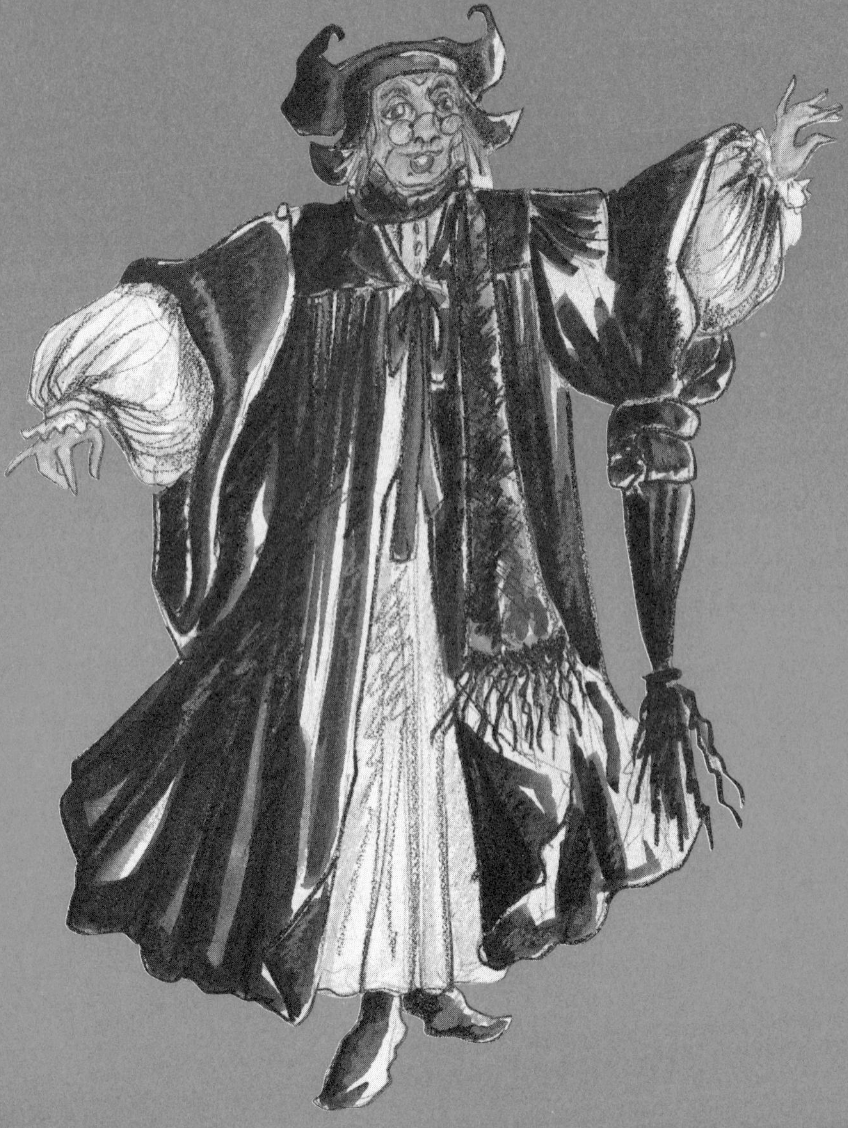

DESSERTS

Chocolate Mousse

SERVES 4 TO 6

4 OUNCES NESTLÉ SEMISWEET CHOCOLATE CHIPS
1 OUNCE BUTTER, UNSALTED
3 EGG YOLKS, FRESH, MEDIUM
2 OUNCES GRANULATED SUGAR
1 CUP HEAVY CREAM

Garnish:
WHIPPED CREAM
WHITE CHOCOLATE PIECES
   OR MILK CHOCOLATE CHIPS

Place chocolate chips and butter in a double boiler. Slowly melt chocolate over low heat. Combine eggs and sugar in a separate bowl and whip by hand or beater. After chocolate has melted, slowly temper the chocolate and butter mixture into the egg mixture. In a chilled mixing bowl, whip heavy cream to firm peaks. Fold chocolate mixture and whipped cream together. Be careful not to deflate cream while folding. Allow filling to set approximately 6 hours in refrigerator before filling glasses. Garnish as desired.

Pat Cleary, Chef
Bristol Bar and Grill

Candide
DOROTHY L. MARSHALL
COSTUME DESIGNER

Be careful not to over-whip the heavy cream. Servings may differ depending on serving glass size.

ACT THREE

Chocolate Pâte with Praline Cream Anglaise

SERVES 10

- 1/4 CUP SUGAR (OR TO TASTE)
- 1/2 CUP WATER
- 8 OUNCES SEMISWEET CHOCOLATE, COARSELY CHOPPED
- 4 OUNCES UNSWEETENED CHOCOLATE, COARSELY CHOPPED
- 3 STICKS BUTTER
- 2 CUPS COCOA
- 2 EGGS
- 4 EGG YOLKS
- 2 TABLESPOONS VANILLA
- 3 TABLESPOONS GRAND MARNIER

Serve with Praline Cream Anglaise (see page 29).

Mike Wilson, Chef
Big Sky Cafe

Butter a loaf pan. Line with buttered wax paper extended 2 inches above pan. In a small saucepan, combine sugar and 1/2 cup water. Dissolve over low heat. Set aside to cool. Mix chocolate, butter, and cocoa in double boiler. Stir until smooth. Remove from heat and cool. Whisk cooled sugar with cooled chocolate. Beat eggs and yolks. Add vanilla and Grand Marnier. Whisk in chocolate mixture. Pour into prepared pan and cover with plastic wrap. Refrigerate 12 hours. Partially submerge pan in hot water for 45 seconds. Invert pâte on chilled platter or serving dish. Peel off wax paper when ready to serve. Cut with hot knife.

DESSERTS

Praline Cream Anglaise

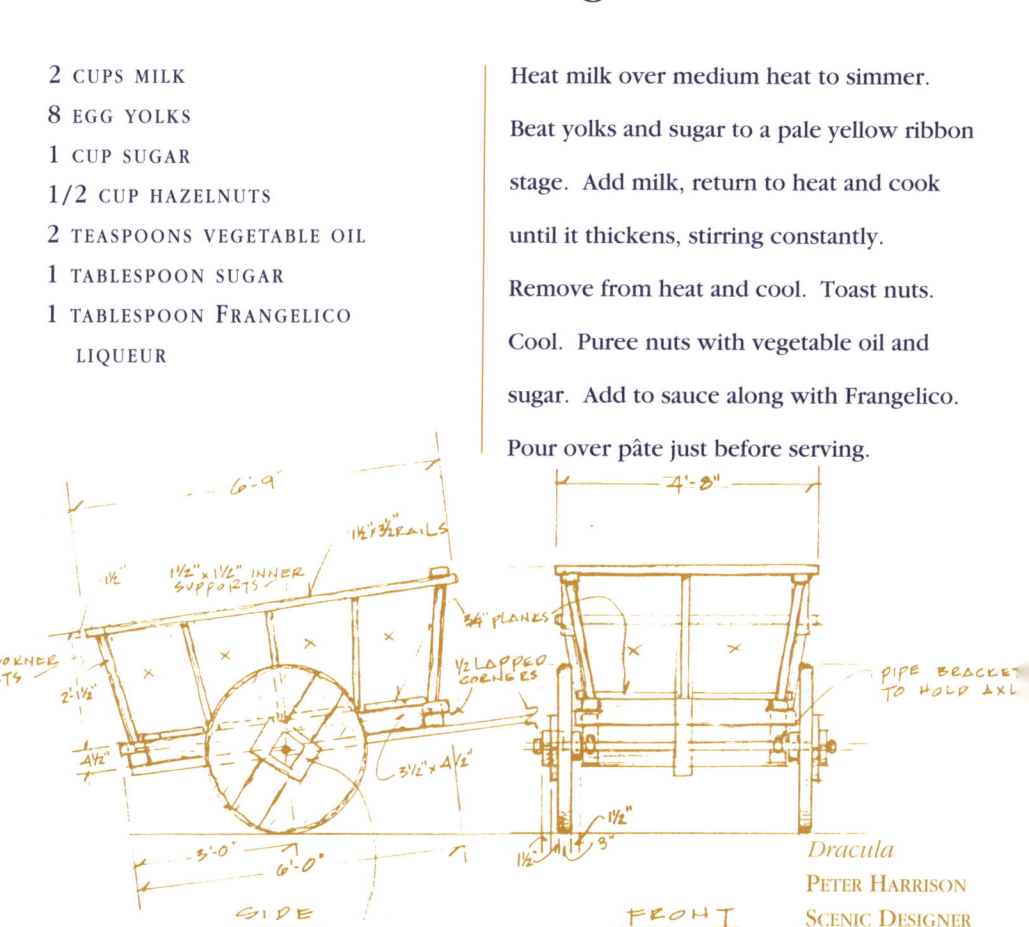

2 CUPS MILK
8 EGG YOLKS
1 CUP SUGAR
1/2 CUP HAZELNUTS
2 TEASPOONS VEGETABLE OIL
1 TABLESPOON SUGAR
1 TABLESPOON FRANGELICO
 LIQUEUR

Heat milk over medium heat to simmer. Beat yolks and sugar to a pale yellow ribbon stage. Add milk, return to heat and cook until it thickens, stirring constantly. Remove from heat and cool. Toast nuts. Cool. Puree nuts with vegetable oil and sugar. Add to sauce along with Frangelico. Pour over pâte just before serving.

Dracula
PETER HARRISON
SCENIC DESIGNER

29

ACT THREE
Chocolate Truffle Cake

16 ounces semisweet chocolate
1/2 cup unsalted butter, (1 stick)
1 1/2 teaspoons flour
1 1/2 teaspoons sugar
1 teaspoon hot water
4 eggs, separated

David Schwartz, Chef
Blayney Catering

Preheat oven to 425 degrees. Grease 8 inch springform pan. Melt chocolate and butter. Add flour, sugar, and water. Blend. Add yolks, one at a time. Beat well. Beat egg whites untill stiff. Fold into chocolate mixture. Bake 15 minutes. Cool before serving.

"Have some chocolates, Eliza."

Pygmalion
George Bernard Shaw

DESSERTS

Chocolate Truffles

MAKES ABOUT 2 DOZEN

12 OUNCES CHOCOLATE, MELTED
4 EGG YOLKS
1/4 CUP HEAVY CREAM
1 STICK BUTTER
3 TABLESPOONS FRAMBOISE OR CHAMBORD LIQUEUR
4 OUNCES CRUSHED HAZELNUTS

Mix all ingredients together and pour into a long cake pan. Chill until firm. Using a small ice cream scoop or soup spoon, roll into balls and then roll in crushed nuts.

*Kathy Schmidt
and Rob Hodes, Chefs
Seven Gables Inn
Bernard's Bar and Bistro*

Pygmalion
JEFFREY STRUCKMAN
COSTUME DESIGNER

ACT THREE

Mini-Truffle Cake with Chocolate Ganache and Fresh Raspberries

30 MINI-CAKES

"At length I recollected the thoughtless saying of a great princess, who, on being informed that the country people had no bread, replied, *'Let them eat cake.'*"

ROUSSEAU

Truffle Cake:

1 POUND SEMISWEET CHOCOLATE CHIPS
10 TABLESPOONS UNSALTED BUTTER
4 WHOLE EGGS
1 TABLESPOON SUGAR
1 TABLESPOON ALL-PURPOSE FOUR
1 TABLESPOON AMARETTO

Chocolate Ganache:

1/2 CUP SEMISWEET CHOCOLATE CHIPS
1/2 CUP HEAVY CREAM
1 TEASPOON VANILLA EXTRACT
1/2 PINT OF FRESH RED OR GOLDEN RASPBERRIES

Gregg Mosberger, Chef
Gregory's Creative Cuisine, Inc.

DESSERTS

Truffle Cake:

Combine chocolate and butter; cook over a double boiler until smooth. Combine eggs and sugar; cook over a double boiler, stirring constantly, until tepid. Remove egg mixture from heat and whip until thick and pale. Fold the flour into the egg mixture. Fold 1/4 egg mixture into the chocolate. Fold the chocolate mixture into the remaining egg mixture and add Amaretto. Pour batter into a prepared 9 x 9 inch baking dish and bake at 425 degrees for approximately 20 minutes. After removing from oven, refrigerate until firm. Cut 1 1/2-inch round circles out of the cake and refrigerate them.

Chocolate Ganache:

Put chocolate chips into a small stainless bowl and set aside. Combine heavy cream and vanilla in a small saucepan and heat until the mixture begins to reach a boil. Slowly pour the hot cream over the chocolate, trying to cover it all. Let stand for one minute and then mix until smooth. Refrigerate the ganache several hours or until firm. Using a pastry bag with a small decorative tip, pipe small circles of ganache onto each of the mini-truffle cakes. Place a fresh raspberry in the center of each circle of ganache and refrigerate until needed.

Suggested wine: Syrah or an Australian Shiraz

ACT THREE

Warm Chocolate and Chestnut Torte

SERVES 8

4 OUNCES SEMIBITTERSWEET CHOCOLATE
4 OUNCES BUTTER
4 LARGE EGGS, SEPARATED
8 OUNCES CHESTNUT PUREE
1/4 TEASPOON VANILLA
1 OUNCE FLOUR
2 OUNCES SUGAR
VANILLA ICE CREAM

Melt chocolate and butter over a double boiler. In a bowl, mix egg yolks, chestnut puree, vanilla, and flour. Fold in chocolate and set aside. Whip egg whites to form peaks. Add sugar while mixing. Fold in 1/3 egg white to base. Fold in remaining whites. Pour batter into 8 x 2 inch round pan. Bake in a 350-degree preheated oven for 30 to 40 minutes. Let cool for 15 minutes before removing from pan. Serve warm with vanilla ice cream.

*Suggested wine:
Bual or Malmsey Madeira*

*David Timmey
Balaban's*

DESSERTS

White Chocolate Cheesecake

SERVES 10

Crust:

2 CUPS GRAHAM CRACKER CRUMBS
1/4 CUP SUGAR
1 TEASPOON CINNAMON
1/2 CUP BUTTER

Filling:

2 POUNDS CREAM CHEESE
   (ROOM TEMPERATURE)
1 CUP SUGAR
6 OUNCES WHITE CHOCOLATE
1 OUNCE CASSIS
4 EGGS

Topping:

1 1/2 CUPS SOUR CREAM
1/3 CUP SUGAR
1/2 TEASPOON VANILLA

Crust: Mix together and press into 10 inch springform pan. Bake 10 minutes at 350 degrees. (Cover outside of springform pan with aluminum wrap.)

Filling: Beat cream cheese and sugar until fluffy. Add chocolate and cassis; mix until smooth. Add eggs one at a time. Mix just until smooth. Pour into prepared crust. Bake 45 minutes at 350 degrees or until set around edges and slightly soft in middle. Cool slightly. Top with sour-cream mixture and return to oven for 5 minutes. Refrigerate overnight for best results.

Topping: Beat together sour cream, sugar, and vanilla until *very* smooth.

Mike Wilson, Chef
Big Sky Cafe

ACT THREE

Double Chocolate Terrine

SERVES 8

- 1 CUP FINELY CHOPPED WALNUTS
- 12 OUNCES SEMISWEET CHOCOLATE
- 3/4 CUP UNSALTED BUTTER
- 3 TABLESPOONS COCOA
- 1/3 CUP SUGAR
- 4 EGG YOLKS
- 5 EGG WHITES, BEATEN UNTIL STIFF WITH A PINCH OF SALT

David Schwartz, Chef
Blayney Catering

Butter a 1 quart loaf pan and line the bottom with parchment paper. Cover bottom with walnuts, and press nuts onto side as high as possible. Set aside. Melt chocolate, butter, and cocoa over low heat in a saucepan or double boiler. Stir until blended. Let cool, but do not allow to harden. Transfer to mixing bowl and beat in sugar. Add egg yolks, one at a time, beating after each addition. Fold in egg whites. Pour mixture into prepared pan. Refrigerate until well chilled. To serve, run a knife around the edges and invert on platter. Let stand at room temperature for 1 hour before serving.

DESSERTS

Chocolate Bread Pudding

SERVES 10

- 1 TABLESPOON BUTTER
- 2 TABLESPOONS FINE BREAD CRUMBS
- 6 OUNCES DARK CHOCOLATE, BITTERSWEET (OR SEMISWEET IF YOU PREFER)
- 2 CUPS MILK
- 4 EGGS
- 1/2 CUP SUGAR
- 8 OUNCES CRUSTLESS BREAD, CUBED (ABOUT 10 SLICES)

Mike Wilson, Chef
Big Sky Cafe

Butter 8 inch springform pan. Dust with bread crumbs and shake out excess. Wrap the bottom and side of pan with foil to prevent seepage. Mix chocolate and milk in saucepan. Warm over medium heat and stir until smooth. Whisk eggs and sugar until smooth. Gradually add chocolate. Fold in crustless bread. Pour into prepared pan and cover with buttered foil. Bake in a water bath in 300-degree oven for 45 minutes. It should be wobbly in the middle. Let cool 20 minutes and serve warm.

"The proof of the pudding *is in the eating."*

Don Quixote
CERVANTES

ACT THREE

Fresh Fruit Cobbler with Vanilla Bean Sauce

MAKES 4 INDIVIDUAL PORTIONS

- 3 CUPS FRUIT OF CHOICE
- 2 CUPS ALL-PURPOSE FLOUR
- 1 TABLESPOON PLUS 1 TEASPOON BAKING POWDER
- 2 CUPS SUGAR
- 4 EGGS
- 1 1/2 CUPS MILK
- 2 TEASPOONS VANILLA EXTRACT
- 2 TEASPOONS LEMON RIND, GRATED

Preheat oven to 350 degrees. Toss the fruit of your choice in a small amount of sugar. Place an even layer of fruit in the bottom of 4 10-inch round soufflé-type dishes. Sift flour and baking powder together into a bowl. Add sugar, eggs, milk, vanilla, and lemon rind, and beat until just combined. Pour 6 ounces of batter over fruit in each soufflé dish until just covered. Bake 30 to 40 minutes or until golden brown.

Serve warm with Vanilla Bean Sauce (see page 39).

Thierry Meignein, Pastry Chef
The Ritz-Carlton, St. Louis

DESSERTS

Vanilla Bean Sauce

1 CUP WHIPPING CREAM
1 VANILLA BEAN, SPLIT LENGTHWISE
6 EGG YOLKS
2 OUNCES GRANULATED SUGAR

Heat cream and vanilla bean to near boiling and remove vanilla bean. Combine yolks and sugar in a bowl and slowly add cream mixture. Pour mixture into a double boiler and slowly stir over medium heat until sauce coats the back of the spoon. Do not over-cook.

The Matchmaker
DOROTHY L. MARSHALL
COSTUME DESIGNER

ACT THREE

Tropical Fruit Shortcake

SERVES 12

For Shortcake:

1 1/2 CUPS FLOUR
1/2 CUP CORNMEAL
1/2 TEASPOON SALT
1 TABLESPOON BAKING POWDER
2 TABLESPOONS SUGAR
1 TEASPOON POPPY SEEDS
1/2 CUP BUTTER
3/4 CUP PLUS 2 TABLESPOONS BUTTERMILK

To Assemble:

2 PINTS STRAWBERRIES, HULLED, CUT IN QUARTERS
2 KIWIS, CUBED
1/2 PINEAPPLE, DICED
1 BANANA, SLICED
2 MANGOES, PITTED AND DICED

Whipped Cream:

2 CUPS HEAVY CREAM*
3 TABLESPOONS POWDERED SUGAR*
  * BEATEN UNTIL STIFF
MINT SPRIG (OPTIONAL)

Combine flour, cornmeal, salt, baking powder, sugar, and poppy seeds. Cut butter into flour mixture to resemble pea-sized shapes; add buttermilk and stir until mixture pulls from side of bowl. Transfer to floured work surface. Roll out to 1-inch thickness. Cut into desired shape. Place on cookie sheet, and brush with buttermilk (may sprinkle with sugar). Bake in preheated 400-degree oven for 10 to 12 minutes or until golden brown. To serve, split shortcake in two; layer fruit and whipped cream. Garnish with fruit and mint sprig.

Suggested wine: Muscatel

Chris Desens
The Country Club at The Legends

DESSERTS

Melted Brie with Winter Fruits

SERVES 12

3/4 CUPS PITTED DATES

1 *EACH* SMALL APPLE AND SMALL FIRM-RIPE PEAR, PEELED, CORED AND DICED

1/2 CUP CURRANTS

1/2 CUP PECANS, CHOPPED

1/3 CUP APPLE JUICE OR APPLE CIDER

1 LARGE WHEEL RIPE BRIE (ABOUT 2 POUNDS), WELL-CHILLED

THIN BAGUETTE SLICES, TOASTED, IF DESIRED.

Brie slices more easily if it is very cold. You can put it in the freezer for 30 minutes to help with cutting. A serrated knife seems to work best.

In a bowl, mix dates, apple, pear, currants, pecans, and juice. Set aside about 2 hours to soften fruit. Cut Brie in half to make 2 round layers. Place 1 layer, cut side up, in an attractive 10-inch shallow-rimmed baking dish (such as a quiche pan). Spread cut side with 2 1/4 cups fruit. Place remaining cheese layer, cut side down, on fruit. Spoon remaining fruit onto center of cheese. (If made ahead, cover and chill filled cheese round up to 2 days.) Bake Brie, uncovered, in 350-degree oven until it melts at edges and center is warm, about 20 minutes. Offer hot Brie from baking dish; scoop up cheese with knife to spread on bread.

Linda Pilcher, Chef
Something Elegant Catering

ACT THREE

Toasted Pound Cake with Fresh Berries Tossed in Rum Syrup

SERVES 12

Rum Syrup:

1 CUP SUGAR
1 CUP RUM (WHITE)
1 CUP WATER

24 SLICES POUND CAKE, SLICED 1/4 INCH THICK
1/2 PINT RASPBERRIES
1/2 PINT BLUEBERRIES
1/2 PINT BLACKBERRIES
1/2 PINT STRAWBERRIES (HALVED)

Rum Syrup:

Place all ingredients in a sauce pot. Bring to a boil. Let boil for about 5 minutes. Transfer to another container and refrigerate. Place pound cake on cookie sheet and toast in 350-degree oven about 8 minutes until golden brown. Put all berries in a bowl and toss with rum syrup. Place 2 pieces of pound cake on each plate and spoon berries over top of cake. Garnish with mint sprig or whipped cream.

Lisa Slay, Chef
Blue Water Grill

DESSERTS

Walnut Pear Mousse with Raspberries

SERVES 4

8 OUNCES SHREDDED FRESH PEAR (2 TO 3 PEARS)
6 OUNCES BLACK WALNUTS, FINELY GROUND
1 OUNCE MELTED SWEET BUTTER
3 OUNCES BROWN SUGAR
CINNAMON TO TASTE
VANILLA TO TASTE
2 CUPS HEAVY CREAM
FRESH RASPBERRIES
MINT
CARAMEL SAUCE (OPTIONAL)

Squeeze shredded pear firmly to extract all juice; place in strainer to continue draining. Process walnuts, butter, sugar, cinnamon, and vanilla in food processor until very finely pureed. Fold in pears. Whip cream and fold into mousse. Chill for 1 hour. Serve with fresh raspberries and mint. Caramel sauce is optional.

Suggested wine: Sauternes

Fio Antognini
Fio's Restaurant

ACT THREE

Raspberries Grand Marnier

SERVES 4

- 3 OUNCES SOUR CREAM
- 2 OUNCES BROWN SUGAR
- 2 OUNCES GRAND MARNIER
- 3 PINTS FRESH RASPBERRIES

Mix sour cream, brown sugar, and Grand Marnier in a medium bowl.

Add fresh raspberries.

Put in small dishes.

Chill for 3 to 4 hours.

Jean-Claude Guillossou, Chef L'Auberge Bretonne

Suggested wine: Muscat

DESSERTS

Raspberry Flan

MAKES 12 INDIVIDUAL SERVINGS

10 OUNCES SUGAR
10 OUNCES WATER
4 CUPS MILK
12 WHOLE EGGS
4 EGG YOLKS
4 CUPS SUGAR
2 PINTS RASPBERRIES

Lisa Slay, Chef
Blue Water Grill

In a thick saucepan, mix 10 ounces sugar in water. Bring to a boil until it caramelizes. Then pour into 6-ounce custard cups (about 1 ounce in each). Set aside to let it harden. Bring 4 cups milk to a boil. Mix eggs, yolks, and sugar using a whisk until sugar dissolves. Pour milk in egg mixture while still whisking. Ladle 5 ounces of mixture into each cup. Place 6 to 7 raspberries on top. Place cups in a 2-inch water bath. Bake at 350 degrees for 50 minutes. To check for doneness: stick a small knife in middle of cup; if the knife comes out clean, it is done. Refrigerate and serve.

Almost September
JOHN CARVER SULLIVAN
COSTUME DESIGNER

ACT THREE

Raspberry Brownies

16 BROWNIES

Brownies:

1 CUP UNSALTED BUTTER, ROOM TEMPERATURE
1 1/4 CUPS SUGAR
1/2 CUP FIRMLY PACKED BROWN SUGAR
4 LARGE EGGS
1/2 CUP UNSWEETENED COCOA POWDER
1 TABLESPOON FRAMBOISE (RASPBERRY BRANDY) OR KIRSCH
1 TEASPOON VANILLA EXTRACT
1/4 TEASPOON SALT
1 1/4 CUPS UNBLEACHED ALL-PURPOSE FLOUR
1 HALF-PINT BASKET FRESH RASPBERRIES

Glaze:

4 OUNCES SEMISWEET CHOCOLATE MORSELS
2 TABLESPOONS FRAMBOISE OR KIRSCH
2 TEASPOONS HOT WATER
POWDERED SUGAR

Linda Pilcher, Chef
Something Elegant Catering

Twelfth Night
MARIE ANNE CHIMENT
COSTUME DESIGNER

"CHEWING THE FOOD OF

Brownies: Preheat oven to 325 degrees. Grease 9 x 13 inch pan. Beat butter, sugar, and brown sugar in large bowl until fluffy. Add eggs 1 at a time, beating well after each addition. Stir in cocoa, framboise, vanilla, and salt. Gently mix in flour. Pour batter into prepared pan. Sprinkle raspberries evenly over batter. Bake until tester inserted into center of brownies comes out clean, about 30 minutes. Cool completely in pan on rack.

SWEET AND BITTER FANCY."

Glaze: Combine chocolate, framboise, and water in top of double boiler. Set over barely simmering water and stir until smooth. Cool slightly. Cut brownies into 3 x 2 inch bars. Sift powdered sugar lightly over brownies. Dip fork into glaze and drizzle glaze decoratively over brownies. Let stand until glaze sets, about 30 minutes.

As You Like It
WILLIAM SHAKESPEARE

Can be prepared 8 hours ahead. Cover and store at room temperature. Can be frozen unglazed for up to 2 weeks. Sift powdered sugar over thawed brownies and glaze as directed above.

ACT THREE

Cranberry Fool With Drunken Oranges

SERVES 12 TO 16

Cranberry Fool:

12 OUNCES CRANBERRIES

1 CUP BROWN SUGAR

1/4 CUP GRAND MARNIER

ZEST OF 1 ORANGE

2 CUPS 40 PERCENT HEAVY WHIPPING CREAM

1 TABLESPOON GELATIN, DISSOLVED IN 1/4 CUP HOT WATER

*Drunken Oranges:**

12 WONDERFUL SEEDLESS NAVAL ORANGES (BLOOD ORANGES; JAFFA ORANGES OR MOST SUNKIST WOULD WORK)

1/2 CUP HONEY

1/2 CUP COGNAC

Tim Brennan, Chef
Cravings Gourmet Desserts, Ltd.

A Christmas Carol
JOHN CARVER SULLIVAN
COSTUME DESIGNER

DESSERTS

In a heavy saucepan, melt butter until the milk solid particles turn toasty brown. Quickly add brown sugar and stir. Add the cranberries and the Grand Marnier; cover and cook to a boil. Reduce heat and simmer until half the berries pop. Remove from heat and cool thoroughly. Set aside. When berry mixture has thoroughly cooled, whip the cream until soft peaks begin to form. Make sure the gelatin has dissolved (no granules should be visible; feel it with your fingers). Quickly drizzle dissolved gelatin into the cream and allow to mix only until incorporated. You'll have to work quickly now. Fold the whipped cream into the berry mixture. Allow to chill about 1 hour until gelatin sets. Thoroughly wash and dry orange. Slice each orange into 6 to 8 slices depending on size. Mix honey together with cognac. Pour over oranges and allow to macerate 2 to 6 hours. Do not allow to sit overnight unless you remove the orange rind because the oil in the rind will create a bitter flavor. *Assembly:* Arrange 4 to 6 orange slices on each plate. Add a healthy dollop or 2 of Cranberry Fool.

* Requires some advanced preparation

ACT THREE

Strawberries Champagne Sabayon

SERVES 4

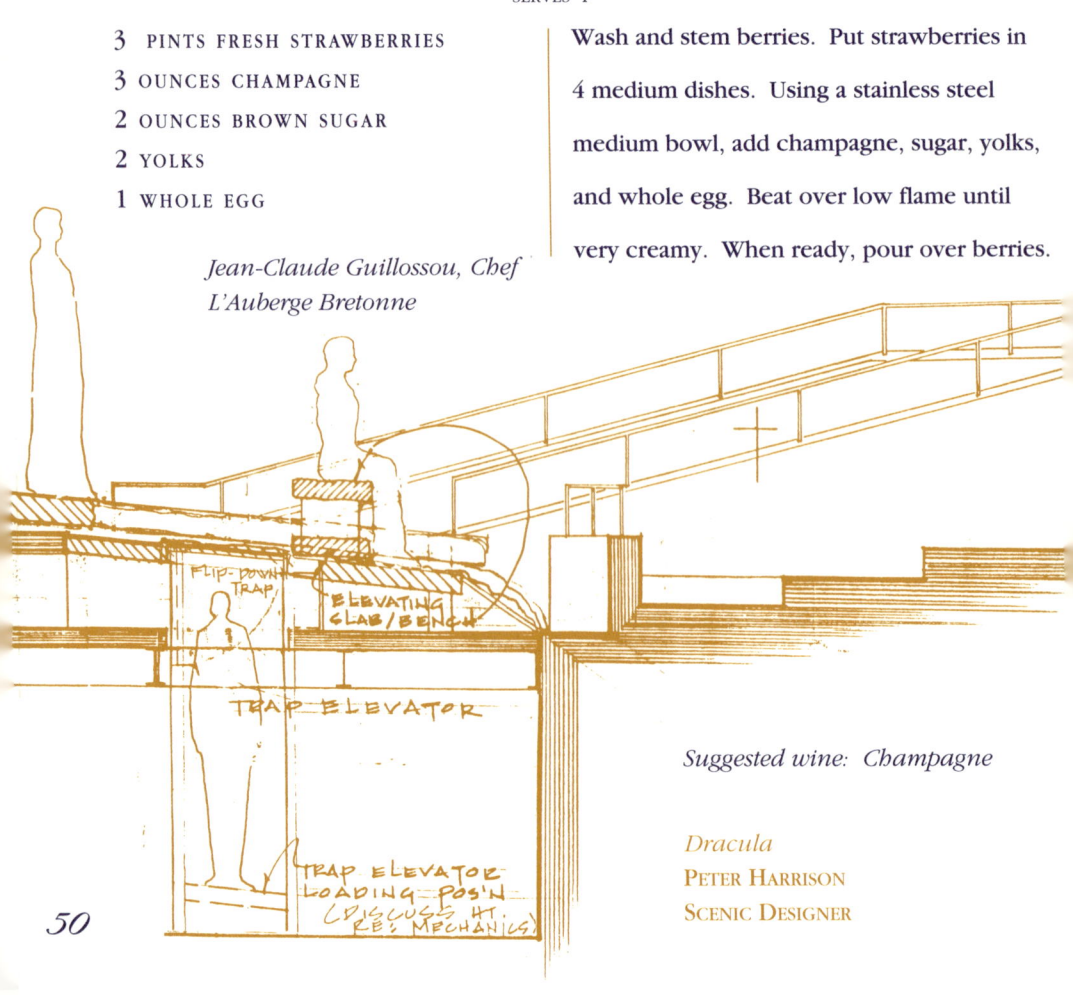

- 3 PINTS FRESH STRAWBERRIES
- 3 OUNCES CHAMPAGNE
- 2 OUNCES BROWN SUGAR
- 2 YOLKS
- 1 WHOLE EGG

Wash and stem berries. Put strawberries in 4 medium dishes. Using a stainless steel medium bowl, add champagne, sugar, yolks, and whole egg. Beat over low flame until very creamy. When ready, pour over berries.

Jean-Claude Guillossou, Chef
L'Auberge Bretonne

Suggested wine: Champagne

Dracula
PETER HARRISON
SCENIC DESIGNER

DESSERTS

Strawberries Italian-Style with Grand Marnier Custard

SERVES 10 TO 12

2 QUARTS FRESH STRAWBERRIES
1/2 CUP ORANGE JUICE
1/2 CUP CHAMPAGNE
1/2 CUP WHITE WINE
1/4 CUP AMARETTO
2 TABLESPOONS SUGAR

Grand Marnier Custard:
1 QUART HALF-AND-HALF
1 CUP SUGAR
4 EGG YOLKS
4 TABLESPOONS GRAND MARNIER

Marinate in refrigerator overnight.

Strain and top with Grand Marnier Custard.

Grand Marnier Custard: Scald half-and-half. Place half of this in a bowl. Add sugar, egg yolks, and Grand Marnier. Mix well and then add back to the sauce pan, stirring constantly. Cook until thick. Do not let it boil or it will curdle. Strain and serve warm or at room temperature.

*Kathy Schmidt
and Rob Hodes, Chefs
Seven Gables Inn
Bernard's Bar and Bistro*

"You will, I trust excuse me that I do not join you; but I have dined already."

Dracula
BRAM STOKER

ACT THREE

Strawberries with Chocolate Dipping Sauce

SERVES 8

2 PINTS STRAWBERRIES, RINSED
1 CUP CREAM CHEESE
1/3 CUP SUGAR, GRANULATED
1/4 CUP WHIPPING CREAM
1/4 CUP SOUR CREAM
CHOCOLATE SAUCE (TO TASTE), PURCHASED OR RECIPE OF YOUR CHOICE

Rinse strawberries and let dry. Combine cream cheese, sugar, whipping cream, and sour cream in an electric mixer. Whip on low for 1 minute, then increase speed slowly to high. Beat for 1 more minute. While mixing on low speed, add chocolate sauce until it reaches desired consistency, texture, and taste. Serve dipping sauce in a bowl alongside berries.

It is simple to prepare these flavors that go so well together.

Suggested wine: Champagne

Chris Desens
The Country Club at The Legends

Strawberry Romanoff

SERVES 4

1 CUP PLUS 3 TABLESPOONS
HALF-AND-HALF
1/2 CUP SUGAR
2 TEASPOONS PLAIN GELATIN
1 CUP SOUR CREAM
1/2 TEASPOON VANILLA

Sauce:
1/4 CUP POWDERED SUGAR
1 1/2 OUNCES VODKA
1 1/2 OUNCES GRAND MARNIER
1 1/2 OUNCES DARK RUM

2 CUPS STRAWBERRIES,* QUARTERED
　You can use any kind of berries.
MINT FOR GARNISH

Mix cream, sugar, and gelatin in saucepan; heat gently until gelatin is dissolved. Cool till slightly thickened. Fold in sour cream and vanilla. Whisk till mixture is smooth. Pour into 4-ounce soufflé cups. Cover and chill till set.

Sauce: Mix powdered sugar, vodka, Grand Marnier, and dark rum. Unmold cream mixture onto plate. Mix strawberries and sauce together. Set for 30 minutes. Pour over gelatin mold. Garnish with mint.

*Suggested wine: Vignoles,
a Missouri grape.*

*Sherrill Gonterman
La Chef Catering*

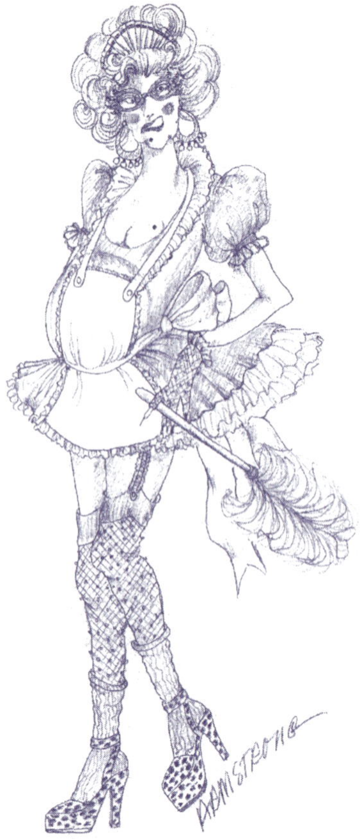
ARMSTRONG

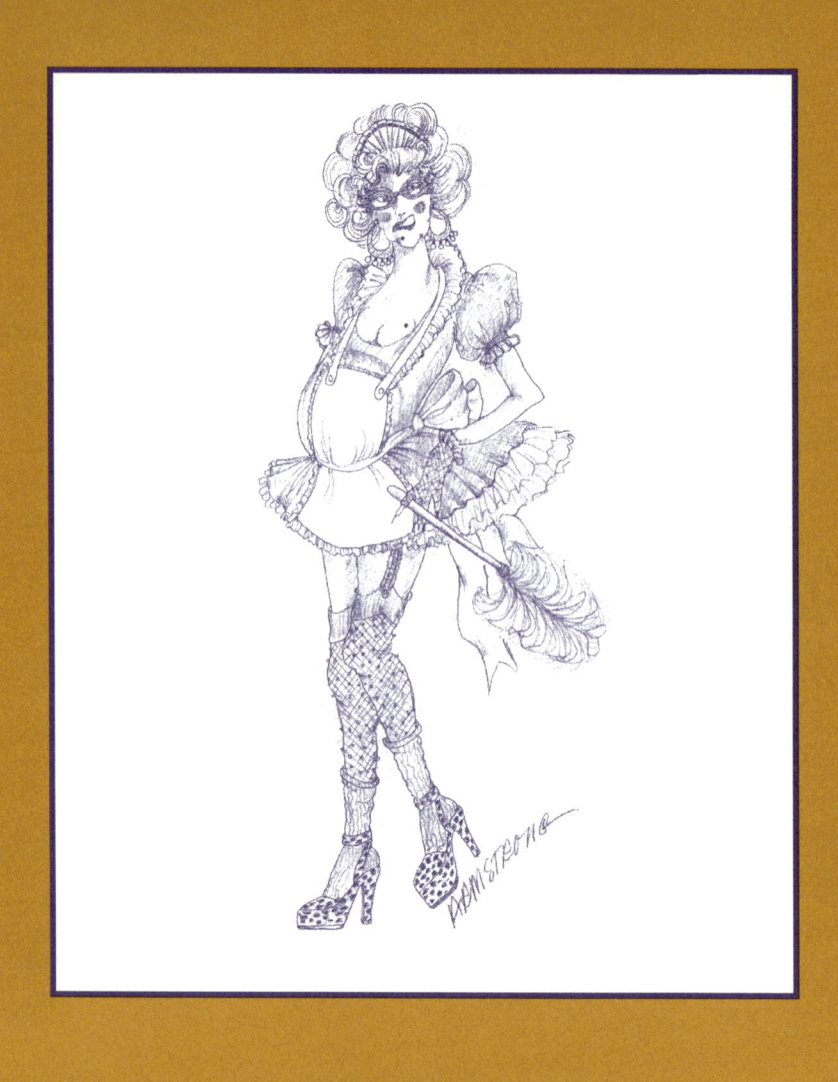

DESSERTS

Strawberry Margarita Pie with Raspberry Sauce

SERVES 10

2 CUPS STRAWBERRIES
10 TABLESPOONS SUGAR
3/4 CUP CONDENSED MILK
7 TABLESPOONS TEQUILA
6 TABLESPOONS TRIPLE SEC
1 TABLESPOON LIME JUICE
2 CUPS CREAM, WHIPPED
1 PREPARED GRAHAM
   CRACKER CRUST

Raspberry Sauce:
2 PINTS RASPBERRIES, FRESH
1/4 CUP SUGAR
2 TABLESPOONS
   CHAMPAGNE VINEGAR

Puree ingredients, fold in cream. Mix gently and pour into a springform pan with a graham cracker crust. Freeze overnight.

Raspberry Sauce: Puree in food processor and strain. Unmold pie, slice and serve with a drizzle of raspberry sauce.

> *The alcohol, which was not cooked in this dessert, is still present!*

*Kathy Schmidt
   and Rob Hodes, Chefs
Seven Gables Inn
Bernard's Bar and Bistro*

A Woman In Mind
ALAN ARMSTRONG
COSTUME DESIGNER

ACT THREE

Roxane's Battle Cake with Chocolate Sour Cream Frosting

SERVES 10

- 3 CUPS SIFTED CAKE FLOUR
- 3 CUPS SUGAR
- 1 CUP COCOA
- 3 TEASPOONS BAKING POWDER
- 1 TEASPOON SALT
- 1 CUP (2 STICKS) BUTTER, SOFTENED
- 1 1/2 CUPS MILK
- 3 TEASPOONS VANILLA
- 3 EGGS
- 1/4 CUP HEAVY CREAM

Serve with Chocolate Sour Cream Frosting (see page 57)

Suggested wine: Cabernet

Jeff Chapman
Cyrano's

In bowl, sift together flour, sugar, cocoa, baking powder, and salt. Make well in center. Add butter, milk, and vanilla. Using electric mixer, beat on low speed until mixed. Stop and scrape bowl. Beat at medium to medium-high speed for 5 minutes. Stop and scrape bowl. Return to low speed to add eggs, 1 at a time, beating 15 seconds after each addition. Add cream and beat 15 seconds. Beat another 15 seconds at medium speed. Pour into 2 greased and floured 8- or 9-inch round cake pans. Bake at 325 degrees for 1 hour 40 minutes or until pick inserted in center comes out clean. Cool cake completely before removing from pan. When cool, frost cake.

DESSERTS

Chocolate Sour Cream Frosting

1 PACKAGE (6 OUNCES) SEMISWEET CHOCOLATE CHIPS (1 CUP)
1/4 CUP BUTTER OR MARGARINE
1/2 CUP DAIRY SOUR CREAM
1 TEASPOON VANILLA
1/4 TEASPOON SALT
2 1/2 CUPS SIFTED CONFECTIONERS' SUGAR

In saucepan over low heat, melt chocolate pieces and butter, stirring frequently. Cool about 10 minutes. Stir in sour cream, vanilla, and salt. Gradually add confectioners' sugar, beating by hand until frosting is smooth and of spreading consistency. Frost top and sides of cake.

This cake was served during the run of Cyrano de Bergerac in The Rep's 1991-92 season.

Cyrano de Bergerac
ALAN ARMSTRONG
COSTUME DESIGNER

ACT THREE

Popcake with Preserves

SERVES 6 TO 8

8 TABLESPOONS BUTTER, UNSALTED
1/2 CUP MILK
1/2 CUP FLOUR
2 EGGS
POWDERED SUGAR FOR DUSTING
LEMON JUICE
PRESERVES OF YOUR CHOICE

Put butter in a 9-inch pie plate or shallow casserole. Place in oven at 475 degrees. Mix milk, flour, and eggs lightly to make a batter. When butter has melted, add batter to the pie plate and bake for 12 minutes. Remove from oven and sprinkle with powdered sugar and lemon juice. Serve with preserves.

David Schwartz, Chef
Blayney Catering

Almost September
JOHN EZELL
SCENIC DESIGN

Tulip Cookies

6 DOZEN COOKIES

2 CUPS SLICED ALMONDS
1 CUP SUGAR
3 EGGS
7 TABLESPOONS MELTED BUTTER
1/4 CUP FLOUR

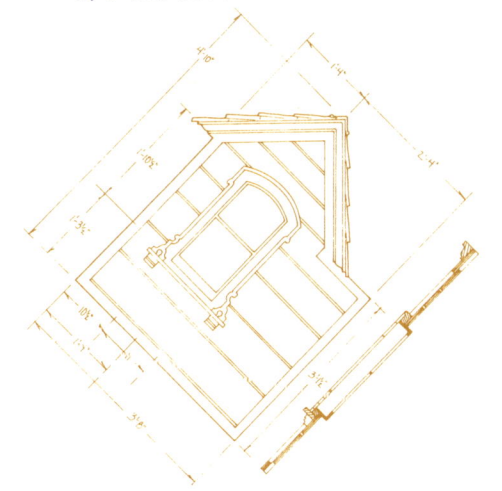

Preheat oven to 375 degrees. Stir together almonds, sugar, eggs, and butter. Mix in flour. Grease and flour a cookie sheet and scoop dough by rounded spoonfuls onto sheet. Dip a fork in cold water and press on dough to flatten. Bake cookies for 8 to 10 minutes or until golden brown.

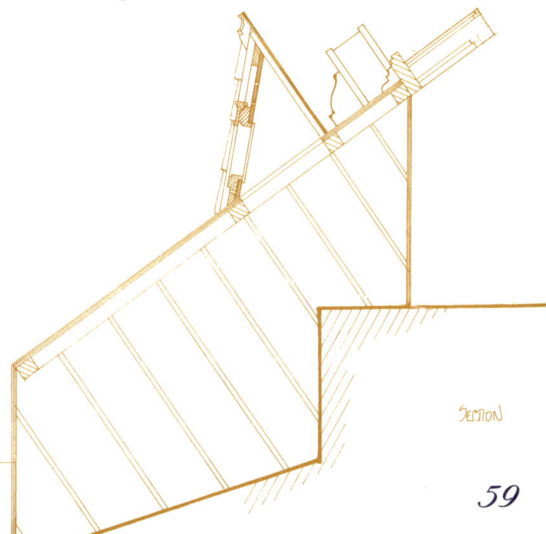

Thierry Meignein, Pastry Chef
The Ritz-Carlton, St. Louis

ACT THREE

Plum Tart

SERVES 6

"Psst...Children... Give me back the bag.

Crust:

1/2 CUP BUTTER

1 CUP SUGAR

1 1/4 CUPS ALL-PURPOSE FLOUR

1/2 TEASPOON SALT

1/2 TEASPOON CINNAMON

1/4 TEASPOON BAKING POWDER

Filling:

1 POUND FRESH PLUMS, FIRM AND TART, WASHED, HALVED, AND PITTED

1 EGG

1 CUP HEAVY CREAM

Linda Pilcher, Chef
Something Elegant Catering

DESSERTS

Cream butter and sugar until fluffy in a food processor. Add rest of dry ingredients and cut until mixture reaches a texture resembling peas (6 to 7 on-off turns). Reserve 1/4 cup of the mixture. Press into 11-inch tart pan. Build up edges a little thicker than bottom. Arrange plums in a single layer over crust, skin side up. Sprinkle with the reserved 1/4 cup crust mixture and bake in a preheated 375-degree oven for 15 minutes. While baking, beat egg slightly in a bowl and add cream. Beat well. Pour egg mixture over plums and return tart to oven for about 25 minutes, or until knife inserted comes out clean. Cool; cut into wedges. Serve warm or cold.

Instead of three pies you shall have six."

Cyrano de Bergerac
EDMOND ROSTAND

ACT THREE

Butterscotch Brownies

SERVES 8

1/4 CUP BUTTER, MELTED
1 CUP BROWN SUGAR
1 EGG
1/2 CUP FLOUR
1 TEASPOON BAKING POWDER
1/2 TEASPOON SALT
1 TEASPOON VANILLA

Melt butter and remove from heat. Stir in sugar. Cool. Beat in egg. Sift flour, baking powder, and salt. Add to mixture. Add vanilla. Pour into greased 8-inch square pan. Bake at 350 degrees for 30 to 40 minutes. Cool; then serve.

David Schwartz, Chef
Blayney Catering

"THE TURNPIKE ROAD TO MOST PEOPLE'S HEARTS, I FIND, LIES THROUGH THEIR MOUTHS, OR I MISTAKE MANKIND."

JOHN WOLCOT

Ginger Brownies

SERVES 8

1/2 POUND UNSALTED BUTTER
1/4 POUND SEMISWEET CHOCOLATE CHIPS
4 WHOLE EGGS
1 1/4 CUPS SUGAR
1 TEASPOON VANILLA
2 TEASPOONS GROUND GINGER
1/2 CUP ALL-PURPOSE FLOUR
1/2 CUP PECANS, CHOPPED

Combine butter and chocolate, and cook over a double boiler until smooth. Combine eggs and sugar in a mixing bowl and whip mixture until thick and pale. Slowly add chocolate mixture to the sugar and eggs. Fold in the remaining ingredients and pour into a buttered 9 x 9 inch pan. Bake at 350 degrees until just set. Let brownies cool and refrigerate.

Suggested wine: Zinfandel

Gregg Mosberger, Chef
Gregory's Creative Cuisine, Inc.

Candide
DOROTHY L. MARSHALL
COSTUME DESIGNER

DESSERTS

Chocolate Pecan Squares

SERVES 16

Pie Dough:

- 2 CUPS ALL-PURPOSE FLOUR
- 1 TEASPOON SALT
- 2/3 CUP BUTTER
- 4 TABLESPOONS COLD WATER

Filling:

- 2 1/2 CUPS DARK CORN SYRUP
- 2 CUPS SUGAR
- 8 WHOLE EGGS
- 8 TABLESPOONS MELTED BUTTER
- 2 TEASPOONS VANILLA EXTRACT
- 4 TABLESPOONS DARK RUM
- 2 CUPS PECANS, CHOPPED
- 2 CUPS SEMISWEET CHOCOLATE CHIPS

Suggested wine: Riesling

Gregg Mosberger, Chef
Gregory's Creative
Cuisine, Inc.

Pie Dough: Combine flour and salt in mixing bowl. Cut butter into flour mixture until it resembles cornmeal in texture. Slowly add the cold water to dough mixture until combined.

Pecan Filling: Combine the corn syrup and sugar in a saucepan and bring to a boil. Stir and cook until sugar is dissolved. Beat the eggs in a mixing bowl. Gradually add the syrup mixture, stirring constantly. Add the remaining ingredients except the pecans and chocolate chips. Sprinkle pecans and chocolate chips into 2 9 x 9 inch pans that have been lined with pie dough. Pour filling into both pans and bake at 350 degrees until golden brown and firm to the touch.

ACT THREE

Classical Coffees

Spirited Coffee BY THE CUP

1 CUP OF COFFEE

   (FLAVORED OR PLAIN)

2 TABLESPOONS OF YOUR FAVORITE LIQUEUR

   (CREME LIQUEUR ESPECIALLY GOOD)

TOP WITH WHIPPED CREAM

DUST WITH COCOA, NUTMEG,

   CINNAMON OR CHOCOLATE SHAVINGS

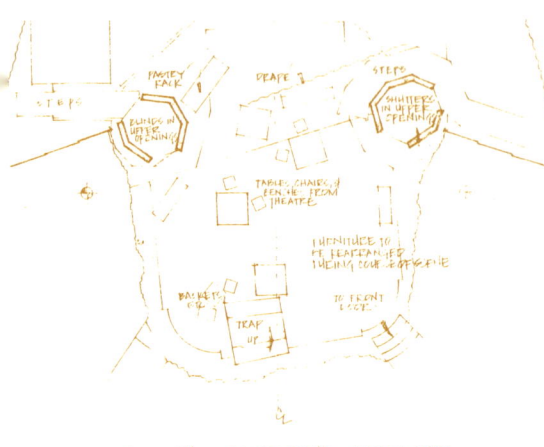

Iced Hazelnut (3 GLASS MUGS)
Blend:

6 OUNCES CREME DE COCOA

2 OUNCES TRIPLE SEC

1/3 CUP POWDERED CREAM

1 TABLESPOON SUGAR

Divide above into 3 mugs –

fill 1/2 to 2/3 with cold hazelnut

coffee. Add ice, stir, serve.

Cyrano de Bergerac
DAVID CRANK
SCENIC DESIGNER

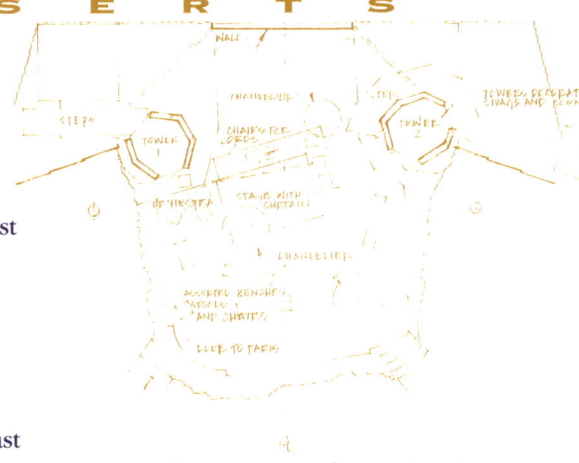

DESSERTS

Serving Suggestions

BREAKFAST – Full-Bodied Dark Roast
   example: Sumatran with French Roast

LUNCH – Sweet Lemon-Flavored Tea or
   Light & Snappy Coffee
   example: Brazilian Santos Coffee

BEFORE DINNER – French or Espresso Roast
   brewed full strength, dilute 1/3 with
   cold water. Serve over ice in a
   stemmed glass with lemon
   twist or sugar.

DINNER

BEEF – heavy, rich, and bold
   example: Celebes Kalossi

FISH – light and mild
   example: Mexican Altura

DESSERT

CHOCOLATE – Decaf, Raspberry,
   Nut, or French Roast

FRUIT – French vanilla

Lois E. Clay
Classical Coffee Company

ACT THREE

Wines

RECOMMENDED BY:

THE CHEESE PLACE, *Amos*

ACT I – *pages 11, 24, 31, 32, 37, 41, 49, 56, 58, 60, 62, 66*

ACT III – *pages 19, 43*

> "YOU DON'T SEE MUCH ELDERBERRY WINE NOWADAYS."
>
> *Arsenic and Old Lace*
> **JOSEPH KESSERLING**

THE WINE CELLAR, *Glenn Bardgett and Geffrey Brooke*

ACT I – *pages 13, 22, 27, 34, 38, 39, 63, 66*

ACT III – *pages 15, 33, 34, 44, 50, 52, 63*

WEST END WINES, *Melanie Harvey and John Sappington*

ACT I – *pages 24, 32, 37, 41, 49, 51, 53, 58, 59, 69*

ACT III – *pages 11, 14, 23, 40, 53, 56, 65*

ACKNOWLEDGMENTS

The Backers Volunteer Board is deeply grateful to all who helped make this publication possible. Our special thanks go to the following people:

PROJECT DIRECTOR:
Beverly Alden Bishop

COPYWRITER:
Bob Mahon

PRODUCTION:
Cheryl McAnally

RESTAURANT/CATERER RECOMMENDATIONS:
Barbara Bridgewater
Mrs. Peter Bunce
Pam and Ed Gomes
Merrell Hansen
Sally C. Johnston
Zoe and Max Lippman
Michael and Rena Murphy
Nancy Forsyth Reed
Glenn Sheffield
Ruth Siteman
Shari Vagnino
Earl E. Walker

COSTUME DESIGNERS:
Alan Armstrong
Marie Anne Chiment
Dorothy L. Marshall
Devon Painter
Jeffrey Struckman
John Carver Sullivan

SCENIC DESIGNERS:
John Ezell
Joel Fontaine
Peter Harrison
Kevin Rupnik
David Crank

THE REP STAFF:
Gordon Alloway
Judy Andrews
Barbara Harris

"May your life be good, like wine — tasty, sharp and clear. And like good wine, may it improve with every passing year."

ITALIAN PROVERB

A Christmas Carol
JOHN CARVER SULLIVAN
COSTUME DESIGNER